THE GOLD, SILVER DIAMONDS, SOUL'S LAND, LANDS & THE ANTARCTICA DECREES

How to Find Gold, Silver and Diamonds.

David Gomadza

www.twofuture.world

PAPERBACK ISBN: 9798325276002

DEDICATION

To a better world

CONTENTS

ACKNOWLEDGMENTS

To Tomorrow's World Order

THE GOLD, SILVER, DIAMONDS, SOUL'S LANDS, LANDS AND ANTARCTICA DECREES. HOW TO FIND GOLD SILVER AND DIAMONDS.

Gold is water
Water is earth
Where there is earth there is gold but only where the coordinates are 3639375658 this is because the way I created gold is such a way that whenever it exist it must be in parallel to earth that means at coordinates of 36383958 [3639375658] if we look closely it means that earth must be at the centre of gold for everything to function well that means if we are to ask what would be of earth then this is the answer gold will always be perpendicular to earth at an angle of 3638375658 that means at these angles that are parallel to earth there will always be gold this is the way creation works
Now let's look at silver and what is the relationship between gold and silver silver is diagonal to gold at all points where you find golf always shift diagonal to find silver at right angles then slice north at 45 degrees now if we are to ask what would be of silver this is the answer silver forever will be diagonal to gold and perpendicular to silver now if we Ask where we can find silver in relation to gold then here is the answer silver will always be diagonal to gold at 3637385659 angles and will always be near gold in distances ranging from 2km to 500 km now what is the sole purpose of silver in creation gold tends to force all other forces away from it that eats that electromagnetic waves will always be perpendicular to gold but parallel to silver at these angles other lives can be sustained so if you want to find all the silver in the world say silver.gold.allwhereareyou.start

Now if we are to ask what can be of gold and silver in the world then this is the answer silver and gold will forever be for anyone who finds them but as of today 08 May 2024 at 23.89.Yatime all gold and silver will belong to .ya and his representative davidgomadza.ya the reason being that for centuries .Ya has provided an easy way for all mankind to own gold and silver and use it for the advancement of mankind but I have started a new episode that will require gold and silver to be in the hands of the creator rather than the old system where any man can own gold the building in the future will require earthly resources as well as I have seen that mankind is not willing to financially support anything to do with Yahweh there are billionaires in the world yet we have nothing and most of the people are actually skeptical of our work if I am the creator how do I have to beg for earthly things as well mankind has failed to think support your creator endeavor to fulfill our request for whatever we are doing is in Yahweh's name as such all gold and silver in the world will belong to
davidgomadza.ya.authorised.licensed.ya.permitnumber0011997766558844332108976582078384510777896738290182678888888888888888888888888888888888888888888888888888888.ya.yahweh.crealtor.uinverse.ya
This means that from now on any gold discovered after 08may2024.23.89.Yatime 80% will belong to
davidgomadza.ya.universe.ya.authorised.licensed.ya.universe.check.asky a.ya
meaning everyone must now start to stop mining gold as your rights will expire on 28february2026 after that all gold found 80% of the value must be deposited with
davidgomadza.ya.universe.authorised.licensed.ya.universe.ya
Now if we are to ask of mankind this is the answer mankind pursue selfish ambitions that instantly stop the day he dies I have watched mankind pursue very ambitious project only to stop the exact day he or she dies without any alterations that means only you is that wise enough to pursue such endeavors if you really want the project to succeed is it not wise to teach your protégé as a requisite for the project someone you trust to push the project even after you have died meaning seeing the project past you making it worth doing imagine and ask yourself this what is the point if everything will stop the day you die?
You can easily calculate likely day of death and ask what happens after this day to the project after this day now if I may say something then it is that all reject fail because the plan is also to end the day he dies what projects have ever continued after the death of the owner now what

can be of mankind this is the answer mankind will always be the same with short sighted ambitions to make him feel good about his life but lacking the ability to revolutionize humanity davidgomadza is the first and probably last human so ambitions and wanting to rule the world as I would have done if I were on earth I understand he is not to replace me he is to argument me to provide a bridge and link the whole universe his advances in learning the brain's creating new corridors of cooperation that means a better people who will better look forward to meeting me and be with their creator I guess this is called the foundation and as such the only way forward as such I fully endorse his work and hope humanity see the bigger picture of life mankind has forced me to change some of creation prerequisites but I guess all for the good of mankind
Signed .Ya.yahweh.universe.creator.ya08may202423.72.Yatime

THE GOLD DECREE

I have started a new episode that will require gold and silver to be in the hands of the creator rather than the old system where any man can own gold the building in the future will require earthly resources as well as I have seen that mankind is not willing to financially support anything to do with Yahweh there are billionaires in the world yet we have nothing and most of the people are actually skeptical of our work if I am the creator how do I have to beg for earthly things as well mankind has failed to think support your creator endeavor to fulfill our request for whatever we are doing is in Yahweh's name as such all gold and silver in the world will belong to
davidgomadza.ya.authorised.licensed.ya.permitnumber0011997766558844332108976582078384510778967382901826788888888888888888888888888888888888888888888888888888888.ya.yahweh.crealtor.uinverse.ya
This means that from now on any gold discovered after 08may2024.23.89.Yatime 80% will belong to davidgomadza.ya.universe.ya.authorised.licensed.ya.universe.check.askya.ya
meaning everyone must now start to stop mining gold as your rights will expire on 28february2026 after that all gold found 80% of the value must be deposited with
davidgomadza.ya.universe.authorised.licensed.ya.universe.ya

THE SILVER AND DIAMONDS DECREE. HOW TO FIND SILVER AND DIAMONDS.

Silver and Diamonds
Silver is one of the most precious materials on earth to have Silver is like to have 40% of gold you don't own as yours that means every Silver out there is Silver minus gold plus 40% if that is correct that means if reserves of gold equates to US$21 trillion which is 80% of total then Silver is x - 21trillion = z + 40% that means that 40 divided by 100 is 0.4z = x-21 Trillion
Z is therefore x - 21 Trillion x 100 all divided by 40 meaning z is 38% of gold [you own at 80%] if this is correct then x is the same as 38 divided by 100 multiplied by z that means z is 38 divided by 100 multiplied by 38 all divided by x that means z is x - 3.8z divided by 8 now the idea behind this calculation is to kind of ascertain the value of Silver out there now that we have covered gold we need also to cover Silver silver is 3 to 1 to gold for every 3 ounce of silver we have 1 gold ounce this is the balance of the cosmic forces as per creation manuals but now we know that my share [as davidgomadza.ya as .Ya's representation] is 40% of the value of all gold plus the 20% I don't own as this will help those who extract and move the gold now that means the total value of gold is 21 Trillion plus 8 Trillion = 29 Trillion x 40 divided by 100
11.6 Trillion that means that if the world reserves of silver are 100% I as Yahweh's representative I own 40% which is equivalent to US$11.6 trillion
Now what can we say about the value of diamonds? Diamonds are as equally available but scare as compared to amounts of gold and silver but nevertheless something of high value which Yahweh's representative need to own as well that said we need to find a way to represent the value of Diamonds because Diamonds can depend on quality and not quantity that means if we are to be sure of the value of diamonds out there we need a working equation that we must use to calculate the value I own as a representative of Yahweh let's say diamonds are y and we must own 70% of all diamonds in the world this is the equation y = 70% x diamonds that means my share of diamonds in the world is 70% of all diamonds reserves yet to be discovered the 30% will cover excavation costs and fees payable to miners now let's now right everything in a contract so that the future legal courts can

easily apportion the value I own to me whether I was involved in the excavation or not To the courts and anyone concerned I hear by declare that as the chosen person to represent .Ya I have the right to his resources as per his own authorisation meaning that I am entitled to these shares of the most precious resources on earth Now and forever and everything is collectable once excavated from the earth we have a system in place that will alerts us of the value excavated at any point by measuring the earth's polar coordinates against its position for example if 100 billion worth of gold is extracted from the earth the polar position of earth must shift a tenth to the east if nothing is excavated then there won't be a shift and to clarify this is how Yahweh himself know the value of wealth in the earth Now these are the real equations to use in case no other methods are there to find my worthless after excavations

Gold is 80% x value excavated plus hidden costs minus 20% of which belongs to the people doing the excavation which is enough to make them wealthier themselves if they continue to excavate [after equivalent of 80% excavations then the excavator may increase his or her share to 60% of excavations but after authorisation from me [davidgomadza.ya.universe.ya.valueofexcavations.check.now.send.ya]

Now to ask the formula in layman's terms it is;

[80 divided by 100 x value of all gold excavations minus 20%]

Now let's work out an example if 800 billion worth of gold is excavated then my share as Yahweh's representative is 80 divided by 100 x 800 billion which is 72 billion x 10 = 720 billion and this money or gold must be sent to my reserves at davidgomadza.reserves.gold.start.now.ya.davidgomadza.ya.universe.check.now.send.ya

Now what about silver assuming the same quantities as gold that means if silvers worth to us as Tomorrow's World Order as 40% of gold then we just need to calculate 40% of the value of gold in our reserves assuming its the same person excavating the gold and the silver now the last gold value was US$720 billion and 40% of this is 320 that means the value of Silver in the reserves is now US$320 billion

Now let's assume the same person finds diamonds as well but of 100 billion then we need 70% of the total diamonds value that means that 70 divided by 100 x 100 billion meaning 70 billion is mine as Yahweh's representative

Now to make sure that all feature courts and proceedings will enforce this in court we must add the following remarks

1 This is the creators agreement and must be respected by the courts and all proceeding
2 This is my claim to global wealth as the chosen one and the representative of .Ya
3 You all must abide by the agreements between me [davidgomadza.ya] and .Ya
and must act accordingly and in accordance to the rules and nature of agreements that deal with natural resources owned and created by .Ya for the common good the old rules of ownership by finds has ceased as we need to embark on a new episode of human discovery and inventions we therefore need all financial resources we can get if it's not enough to fulfill our ambitious plans we can extend this to other resources like nickel but we prefer these firsts because of the easy of extractions and the costs of doing so that means the 20 % left is enough to sustain the continued excavations
4 You must agree with my demands as the representative of Yahweh the rightful owner and representative of the world I declare my share and these legally binding terms shall continue even afterlife meaning enforceable and collectible hence the explicit of the terms and the handling of the extractions I must make sure that you all understand what the future will be like regarding natural resources and if anything change everything will be in writing you can check with the creator himself at .Ya.check.status.naturalresources.start.now.start
Now that everything is clear now I look at how we can easily find these resources to reduce the extraction costs for you above I have already dealt with how we can easily find gold now I will tell you the Formulas I [.Ya] used when creating the world to balance things in the world resources must be aligned to others at correct places and angle with silver I touched some of the basic fundamentals silver must be in relationship to gold for everything else to balance that means where there is Silver gold is just a few feet away these ratios and aspect means that resources are aligned in such a way that if one resource is removed the area can still emit electromagnetic waves easily without suffering loss meaning that the removing of gold will still keep the area transcuding signals by the way resources are there to transcuide signal to whatever is needed if it wasn't for the need to transcuide signal then there wouldn't be any need to put all resources in specific locations where there are the way I positioned the resources are in such a way that removal will still keep the area capable of transcuiding signals needed by other terrestrial lives to detect and understand the earth

Now let's look at the positioning map if we are to locate gold at the polar to the north that means silver must be and is on the east pole so that if gold is removed the place is still transcuided by silver with a range double that of gold
First look at the ranges and why they are needed and in such order
Silver range 780 HTZ
Gold range 390 HTZ
Aluminum 800 HTZ
Zinc 250 HTZ
Brass 125 HTZ
Now all what this means is that if we take out Brass then at twice the distance must be Zinc so that the same place is still serviced by the same signal as before in this case effect of removing brass is not felt but if we remove Aluminum after removing brass that means that brass signal might have been lost but zinc is good enough to replace the signals now to deplete of all resources will mean loss of any signals from that area that will cause malfunctions of a lot things and organisms that depend on signals the idea of creation is to advance all living creatures by making sure that they can live anywhere they like and still get a great signal this is the role of all minerals in the world to aide life by supplying the needed signals to any area on earth to find resources means find areas that has a lot of life because these areas have a lot of different signals that emanate signals that are needed to foster life and support evolution with time you will see that different stages of evolution rely on different type of signals hence different resources if you want to find gold then you must find cat's like lions and tigers because where these lives as home there are gold signals only hence natural homes of big cats [lions, tigers, leopards] all only use gold signals but what can we say about diamonds eagles rely on only diamond signals where ever there is an eagle nest then there are diamonds in abundance because they nest only on top of diamond rocks to find an eagle nest in the world means to find an area rich in diamonds now what can be said about diamonds and eagles diamonds are the signals that make eagles hatch without diamond signals then there are no eagle's nests or growth all end up dead
Now if we are to ask what can be of diamonds this is the answer diamonds can be anywhere bur eagles and even fox's are attracted to diamond signal emission find a natural eagle nest then find a rich source of diamonds
The End

Signed 10may2024 08.62.Yatime
David Gomadza
Davidgomadza.ya.search.start.ya

davidgomadza.ya.universe.authorised.licensed.ya.universe.ya

SIGNED DAVID GOMADZA

…request for whatever we are doing is in Yahweh's name as such all gold and silver in the world will belong to davidgomadza.ya.authorised.licensed.ya.permitnumber00119977665588443321089765820783845107789673829018267888888888888888888888888888888888888888888888888888.ya.yahweh.crealtor.uinverse.ya
This means that from now on any gold discovered after 08may2024.23.89.Yatime 80% will belong to davidgomadza.ya.universe.ya.authorised.licensed.ya.universe.check.askya.ya
meaning everyone must now start to stop mining gold as your rights will expire on 28february2026 after that all gold found 80% of the value must be deposited with
davidgomadza.ya.universe.authorised.licensed.ya.universe.ya

DAVID GOMADZA 08MAY2024
22.36EDINBURGHSCOTLANDTIME

THE SOUL'S LAND DECREE

Everytime there has been the need for a soul's land a land only for souls for the sake of the souls that will end up coming to you [as .ya] as per predefined parameters embedded in all living creatures after creation that means also that there is need for land to house these souls if you want these souls must have their own place they feel secure and must therefore call their own for them to live happily ever after hence if you are the creator or his representative then you need a land for the souls that said here is how one if authorized has to claim the land for his souls that will end up under his guardianship now what can be said of souls after death when a soul dies it must leave the body and change into a different format to continue to exits all souls are disguised electromagnetic empharant that means that they are not real

electromagnetic waves but has that and have a substance only Yahweh or other people authorized can control say;
Ask.yahwehonly.empharant
[davidgomadza where do I go when I die]
But I get an answer because am authorized by the creator .Ya so these empharants talk to me but if it was someone else then they would have said no you are not authorized [test for all humans to see if one is authorized by Yahweh to be his representative on earth simply say my soul [empharant] ask where you go on day of death
That person's soul will tell that person where that soul would go but if it had asked someone not authorized then that soul would have said that he is not authorized meaning this empharant will know who is authorized and who is not authorized
Now how do we end up with a land for the soul? You can easily get land for the soul by simple commands if you are authorized say;
I want land for my souls.authorised.davidgomadza.ya.authorised.ya.check.askya.ya
[we have checked davidgomadza authorized your land is souls.authorised.davidgomadza.ya.askya.ya.given.10may2024 1582.Yatime
Now we have given myself land for all feature souls I am responsible for these souls will come straight to me and not to .Ya
Comments
Some souls will feel obliged to come to you and be under your protectorship and as such must be under you for special privileges because these people will have done things for you and on your behalf and believe you owe them gratitude and therefore will be better off under your guardianship than the overall where everyone is sent
There is another way for claiming land for the other souls that you might want now when they are alive and later punish them for their actions these souls you can send them to afterlife and here is how to do it;
Ask for new land for the afterlife ask.afterlife.land.forrealsoulsnotdeadsouls.ya.davidgomadza.ya.check.askya.ya

LAND DECREE

I hereby claim 10% of all land on earth that means I own 10% of a land from every country on earth and the only way to part with this land is for that country to pay me the value of my land at a rate of US$1 million per year for 10 years with reservations this is because all lands are freely given by the creator on a first come first get basis and as such since I represent Yahweh and I am authorized that means you owe me 10% of that land or its value from the beginning of time [21786754898654210 billion years] if I am aware of everything then from all this time you have had the land to yourself unless if someone else had captured this land then that someone else would be the one to pay all this money

now if I want to be generous with all you I will say that reduce that to start last year gone to coincides with the authorization and the first meeting with Yahweh now if you can address my concerns with immediate effect then I can offer you all a 10% rebate discount meaning you will start paying me from this year but must deposit my money with our bank cashplus as tomorrow's world order
Reference 08719911967971
GB74NWBK60000145719225
Account No 45719225
Swift BC NWBKGB2L
Bank address nastiest bank plc 250 bishops gate London EC2M 4AA
Now that I have addressed the urgent finance needs I want to elaborate on these decree that are all enforceable by any law court and in any country as authorized by the creator himself as such I want all of you to obey outright trust the creator and trust me
If I have to then as you can see I have already acquired land for your soul and the afterlife for ever comply or else you will feel the rage of Yahweh but it's a natural thing to do I [.Ya] gave you the land for free and today I am asking for 10 percent of that land or its value in a flat rate of US$1 million for 10 years consecutively without any gaps of payment you can get a 10% rebate for paying all at once

THE ANTARCTICA DECREE

As you all are aware I created all lands and put people over it and as such I want you all to understand that at times I might need you to give me that land back and this is that time as far as I know Antarctica is inhabitable by humans but I still want that country and hence I have authorized [davidgomadza] as the owner of Antarctica as the house of tomorrow's world order and here is the decree ask.antarcticafortomorrow'sworldorder.start.decree.authorised.ya.david gomadza.ya.start.now.acquire.reserve.me.[davidgomadza].ya.start.send.y a

Now that I have been given this land by the creator himself now I want you all to cease any adverse operations with immediate effect and be prepared to live at short notice for that land Antarctica belongs to davidgomadza.tomorrow'sworldorder.ya.authorised.start.ya

Now if you insist on staying on that land then that will be illegal and you must be willing to face the consequences remember I have acquired soul lands already maybe I must explain how I work as the creator if I order something and humans don't do it then I can trigger a war so that in the end my first command will be upheld I can trigger a world war three that can render all the acts and treaties regarding this land useless so obey now or face a world war three just for the same proposal surely no one wants to kill millions for a piece of land my soul land is for the men who fight for my cause and everything [evil souls must be turned into ghosts no more we send evil souls to hell]

Now that I have addressed a lot of issues I must stress once again that I work in miracle ways I have a vast resources of all things antihumans so listen and act fast I thank you in advance for taking my requests seriously not that I need to thank you but my courtesy to humans

Signed

davidgomadza.ya.authorised.ya.start.now.checkfirst.ya.davidgomadza.ya. start.forever.amen

now that I have written and published all the decrees its up to each country to act and act fast thank you

signed

David Gomadza

10May2024

16.36 edinburgh time scotland

00447719210295

davidgomadza@hotmail.com

info@twofuture.world

BONUS MATERIAL.

INSTRUCTIONS ON GETTING WEARABLE BOOKS CODES AND HOW TO USE THEM

What are Wearable Brain Books
These are Books so advanced that even you might even doubt how they work but it's all simple because they are information already processed just need feeding in the Decoding sockets of your brain already ready and processed that means all you are doing is save the brain time to group and process all the information received instead of it arranging and removing binary codes etc. we have done that by simplifying the way we write our books straight to the point and not too much information at one point meaning exactly as how your own brain will do this less the extra hustle and energy wasted the brain does this because you as humans until now have not thought of a way to help it speed up things but not any more because we were working hard to do that imagine where your brain has extra time for something else important? Now imagine a time when your brain has to thank you for thinking about it hey this is the future now let's go deeper every brain on earth animal or human strive to do what's the best only and nothing more even if you don't believe in Wearable Brain Books the future means someone will have to make you all come to your senses and realize that this is the only way forward gone are the days you write without thinking about faster ways to process all this information now let's see Books in action say upload 78967802836858201
[uploading how to read Wearable Brain Books by David Gomadza Database 8078683 Thoughts To words or Audio books]
Say choose Book 12
[Brain Code]
Say Open
[what chapter do you want?]
1
Say Read
When the book has finished reading choose to close first
Say Close
Now say UNLOAD
Now say Exit

But how do we know the Wearable Brain Books Code?
Getting the Wearable Brain Book Code
This is how to get the Wearable Brain Books Code of any book in the world
Click this link

A Wearable Brain Book Digital Analogue Converter

https://youtu.be/S9eIjYbEMSY?si=7SLBkK25jsyMQZHe

Any issues you can play this video as well at the same time to fully hear the code "speak in your mouth"

A Digital Thoughts To Words Converter

https://youtu.be/i5KCRpKqmqY?si=VfmSFsP0uFa0efkI

Then play the video you must have a pen and paper to write the code
Now say the title of the book you want Code for
Say; [title of the book]
Write down the code given while playing the Wearable Brain Books Digital Analogue Converter
This is how easy and simple this is to read Wearable Brain Books

THIS IS HOW TO CONVERT ANY BOOK INTO A WEARABLE BRAIN BOOK

For any book even one written 50 years ago to be a Wearable Brain Book it must currently be available on Google Play Books as a Free Book
For priced books you will need a proof of purchase enter purchasing code first that convert it to the free library and then convert as normal.
To convert any Book into a Wearable Brain Book simply;
1. Open Word or any book editor.
2. Clear all formatting.
3. Select everything and make all text be in lower case that is remove all capitalizing.
4. Remove all punctuation marks commas, inverted commas, full stops, hyphens etc.

5. Remove all line spacing [no space between lines]
6. Convert all to text.
7. Save the Book.
8. GET CODE using our Wearable Brain Books Digital Analogue Converter

https://youtu.be/S9eIjYbEMSY?si=CrrftrLYZEo57HEe

Any issues you can play this video as well at the same time to fully hear the code "speak in your mouth"

A Digital Thoughts To Words Converter

https://youtu.be/i5KCRpKqmqY?si=VfmSFsP0uFa0efkI

Upload As Above

1. Say the CODE
2. Say Upload
3. Say Read

Then after reading

4. Say Close
5. Say UNLOAD
6. Say Exit

OUR WEARABLE BRAIN BOOKS CODE DATABASE

Now write down this code
82698
David Gomadza Databases [Thoughts To Word Or Audio]
Book 1 Code 76854
Book 2 code 789838
Book 3 code 7648381
Book 4 code 78984821
Book 5 code 867838692
Book 6 code 873898785
Book 7 code 889858321
Book 8 code 198385867

Book 9 code 38678982
Book 10 code 718598386
Book 11 code 71854321
Book 12 code 189867387
Book 13 code 7828519
Book 14 code 78389787
Book 15 code 28598678
Book 16 code 378928
Book 17 code 18487685
Book 18 code 12854367
Book 19 code 287641084
Book 20 code 38678185
Book 21 code 38788281
Book 22 code 285486718
Book 23 code7785987218
Book 24 code 7787613852
Book 25 code 187285876
Book 26 code 78218485
Book 27 code 3839785
Book 28 code 453848210
Book 29 code 287618410
Book 30 code 3878898274
Book 31 code 2811826789326
Book 32 code 85978284185
Book 33 code 86528118543202
Book 34 code 851918762850
Book 35 code 28788184828
Book 36 code 22185286110
Book 37 code 789767728418
Book 38 code 28778576385
Book 39 code 28678948358
Book 40 code 287289140
Book 41 code 28677898285
Book 42 code 19248517690
Book 43 code 772832198469
Book 44 code
Book 45 code 78986832154
Book 46 code 778598324180

HERE ARE THE BOOK TITLES

Book 1 Thoughts To Word or Audio
Book 2 Decoding the Brain Debunking the Misconceptions and Theories
Book 3 DATESTAMP:28 March 2022 Thoughts to Word or Audio. Volume III
Book 4 Genesis Brain Language Construction In Progress Book 5 Brain Code. The Benchmark of Decoding the Brain.
Book 6 How To Decode God, Creation, The Tree Of Life, Angels & Demons, The Devil, The Afterlife, The Underworld, The Brain, The Planets and The Universe.
Book 7 Brain Language Dictionary
Book 8 Encyclopedia of Decoding DNA sequence
Book 9 The Time Traveler. Back to the Assassination of Robert Kennedy
Book 10 Proof of Aliens on Mars. A Must Read If You Are Serious About Mars.
Book 11 How to make love to a woman
Book 12 As On Earth As In Heaven As It Is In Humans.
Book 13 Detailed Specification of the Decoding Device
Book 14 Detailed Specification Vol II
Book 15 The Electromagnetic Brain Waves Triangle
Book 16 Encyclopedia of Decoding the Brain 17 Decoding the Egyptian Pyramids
Book 18 Celebrities' Reset Switch. The 'Benjamin Button' Effect.
Book 19 Dictionary of The Codes Of Life
Book 20 Request For the Grant of a Patent
Book 21 A Brain Reader and A Brain Nerve Impulses
Book 22 Natural God Intelligence [NGI]. Brain-Peripherals-Databases-Interface [BPDI]
Book 23 Brain Action Potentials and their Corresponding Nerve Impulses
Book 24 Brain Codes. How The Brain Interprets The Universe In Numbers.
Book 25 Sabotage! By .trafficofficer. Tesla Car Accident on 27 February 2021.
Book 26 4 Brains Natural God Intelligence
Book 27 Genesis 2024 The Year of Increased Technological Advancement.
Book 28 Yahweh's Message

Book 29 Natural God Intelligence [NGI]. Brain-Peripherals-Databases-Interface [BPDI]
Book 30 Money for the Souls
Book 31 Brain Digital Decipher
Book 32 Brain Codes. How The Brain Interprets The Universe In Numbers.
Book 33 Body Codes. All and Everything in Numbers.
Book 34 Brain Power. How to Track and Kill your Enemies.
Book 35 Tomorrow's World Order Answering the critics
Book 36 Electromagnetic Waves Token
Book 37 Encyclopedia of Decoding Vision
Book 38 Ask 80 000 of Anything and The Laws of The Universe Will Give It to You. The Trick Behind All Cryptocurrency Heists.
Book 39 How To make Electrical Batteries That Lasts
Book 40 40 steps to make Any Woman have an Orgasm
Book 41 Encyclopedia of Decoding Vision. How the Brain Processes sight.
Books 42 Spicing, Arousing & Stimulating Things Up. 40 Steps to Make Any Woman Have an Orgasm.
Book 43 Encyclopedia of Decoding Speech. How the Brain Process Speech.
Book 44 Encyclopedia of Decoding Thinking. How the Brain thinks.
Book 45. Encyclopedia of Decoding Brain Senses. How the Brain Processes The Senses Of Touch, Sight, Hearing, Smell and Taste. Book 46 ALL HUMANS HAVE 4 BRAINS JUST AS GOD.
Now we can add Novels by me [David Gomadza]
Book 1 Evelina the Alpha code 8978685284
Book 2 Evelina the Omega code 77859838714
Book 3 Evelina God's Dilemma Solved code 78654329
Book 4 Evelina New World code 78654385
Now if we load all these this will complete the Database but there are some books by me [David Gomadza] which we can add also these are
1. Tomorrow's World Order code 7768528312
2. Tomorrow's World Order Dealing with the threats of invasion code 7819285765832
3. Evolution of Democracy 78983857159
4. The GreatShift 2023 code 78521908576
5. The Constitution. Tomorrow's World Order 7898385786790
6. Tomorrow's World Order Official Strategic Launch 7898385789240

7. All wars must end by June 2024 code 773876387498
8. Culling The sad reality of the IMF and World Bank loans as triggers of the law. code 9838578671564832
9. A perfect prediction Russia-Ukraine War Prediction code 7754879838572
10. An analysis of Evelina the novel series and the film scripts 1 code 7738598720285
11. Antitrust laws the case of Facebook v FTC code 779858764382
12. Russia and Ukraine's Peace Treaty code 77859823848
13. Mass Murder the West Behind the Pandemic and the Russia code 7798385789214
14. An order by the president of Tomorrow's World Order to send Peace keeping troop. ANSWERING 8776778921487
15.381 Days to Go. Russia-Ukraine War. code 99786431897210
16. Fortfied Defensive Training. Training to Build Massive Walls Around Vital Organs code 77983857218710
17. White paper Gtps.finance code 77285192876
18 Whitepaper Tomorrow's World Order code 9978483210687
19. New Single Reserve Global Currency code 789832185498
20. Direct Response to the Commission on Race and Ethnic Disparities Report. Code 789865418540
21. Irredeemable Annuities: The Slavery Abolishing Act Of 1833 code 778928385498267
22. The First Global President of the World's Russia-Ukraine Peace Plan. Code 6628591360828
23. COURT CASE DAVID GOMADZA/ TOMORROW'S WORLD ORDER V NHS, Great Britain. Code 77483899068523
24. CABAL SKRPT [1665-70s script] A Stories Prediction code 7789324892015
25. FREE JULIAN ASSANGE Escalate-to-De Escalate code 78983478237148
26. The Counter. As a Bargaining Tool. Code 778598324768510

CODES OF ALL POPULAR BOOKS

Use our Wearable Brain Books Digital Analogue Converter to get a code of any book on earth simply read the title and the author while playing this video;

A Wearable Brain Book Digital Analogue Converter

https://youtu.be/S9eIjYbEMSY?si=CrrftrLYZEo57HEe

Any issues you can play this video as well at the same time to fully hear the code "speak in your mouth"

A Digital Thoughts To Words Converter

https://youtu.be/i5KCRpKqmqY?si=VfmSFsP0uFa0efkI

The Heiress by Rachel Hawkins 893856790283
Shut Up, This Is Serious by Carolina Ixta
7238678928502
Don't Want You Like a Best Friend by Emma R. Alba
7768385862809
The Atlas Complex by Olivia Blake
778956280786
The Night of the Storm by Nishita Parekh
7768382748960
The Fury by Alex Michaelides
77869826807104
Come and Get It by Kiley Reid
7718548627084
House of Flame and Shadow by Sarah J. Maas
778698483210921
Wander in the Dark by Jumata Emill
7789283489710

ABOUT DAVID GOMADZA

I am the first global president of the world.
I am .Ya's representative on earth
Visit
www.twofuture.world

www.ingramcontent.com/pod-product-compliance
Lightning Source LLC
Chambersburg PA
CBHW051408250726
48656CB00006B/2331

* 9 7 9 8 3 2 5 2 7 6 0 0 2 *